I0164157

Ebook ISBN#: 979-8-9920346-4-6

Paperback ISBN#: 9780981635842

About the Author

A brain tumor survivor since the age of 8, and handicapped since the age of 10, C.R. Reardon is now 39-years-old. He fell in love with creative writing after writing a poem about these hardships in the 7th grade. Since then I have self-published five books: *Born on Friday the 13th* (2018), *Torghatten* (2016), *Hard Polish* (2013), and *Spawning Gray* (2010). After 2 years at The University of Arizona, C.R. graduated from Stonehill College in 2009 and earned my Master's degree in English in 2011 from Salem State University.

His screenplay *Lagom* (the Swedish word for 'just the right amount') was a finalist for best screenplay at the 2017 Massachusetts Independent Film Festival, as well as the 2015 Catalina Film Festival. In 2016 his screenplay *Spawning Neon* was a semi-finalist at the 16th annual Awareness Film Festival.

Recently, he has written articles for *The Guardian*, *The Boston Globe*, *The Verge*, *Wired*, *Gizmodo*, *PC Mag*, *Laptop Magazine*, and *Yes! Magazine*. He also has works in disability literary journals like *Breath & Shadow*, *wordgathering*, and *Deaf Poets Society*.

Torghatten

C.R. Reardon

C.R. Reardon

I. Seeds

Wonder

Sam White sat under a tree with a wish.
He looked over a lake at *Atlantis*:
Strapped to an orange rocket with two white sleighs,
One last time, that ship soared on her way.
In Sam's backyard, while sparks cascaded,
A thunderous roar burgeoned, faded, and,
Like a streaming comet in the night glows,
Sam watched mankind rise as smoke billowed.
That night the celestial gods cried
Because we forgot what brought us to life.
We got to now swimming with the Earth's streams
Leading us to a waterfall of dreams.
Off the lake, Sam saw glory's reflection—
Long live the blaze of imagination!

Cultured

The two sit in a plane:
He listening to guitar riffs
Through plastic wires spewing
From his ears, she
Watching the in-flight movie
Fool's Gold.

Upon arrival, he observes
Unfamiliar fashions
On passing bodies,
Words off a local's
Whiskey-soaked tongue,
The aroma of a vendor's
Greasy cuisine; she
Slices through jostling bodies—
Her pupils fixed on her mark,
Her escape.

After a night's sleep in a posh hotel,
They are driven at 8:45 AM
To a museum where they
Are told about meteorology,
Explained the body's intricate
Systems and canals
As fossils and exhibits
Stare back.
Outside cars speed,
People walk, the Sun
Bursts.

The Wall

Behind the off-white wall
With its radiator along
The baseboard, its two blue
Chest-high cabinets—
The left one's shelves
Slant to the right—
And a creamy, beat-up dresser
Between the cabinets,

The wall's
Mazelike piping operates
In a beautiful geometry
Like electronic wicks
Fulgurating to Semtext.

But behind this wall
Several pipes are pinched, as
Though what they carried
Snapped and
Cannot be fixed.

Withdrawal Pains

His religion will be tested in the morning.
Right now, he screams in bed with the lights off.
A figure rushes in, puts an arm under his knees, behind his back,

And carries the whaling to the other room.
There's an empty, orange bottle in the barrel.
The lights in the room are dim, like dusk.
In the dreamy confusion, an angel wipes the sweat from his forehead,
But the rocks in his knees won't stop exploding.

The Ramp that was Frozen with Ice

Going up a ramp,
When it's cold, wet, snow-blanketed,
Is a cruel climb.
You look for a friend in a rail that you can grab hold of,
But the rail is glazed with ice, unable to provide the help that you
need.
It seems like nature is saying, "Not this one,"
But if you give up and have to come back later,
Chances are the ice will be harder.

Poetry 101

May symbols congeal
And form various combinations
That travel faster than sound
Through synapses, delivering
Them to my tongue,
Activating my vocal cords
So I can talk at you.

A poem is mulled,
Slowly-released from the
Fingertips, translating
The abstract into
A Grecian Urn.

Digital Towers

Disillusioned
By collusion
Among six salesmen
Vying for inclusion
In distribution
Of digital profits—
What a bunch of socialists.

I'm here to tell you, friends,
You don't need them
Renting space on
Your cerebellum.
They complain
Because we're entertained
And they're not in
The picture's frame.

It's a new Monday.
We mail a different way.
Us kids have changed the game,
Deconstructing ivory towers
With a computer
And our brains.
We've constructed digital towers.

Family Cookout at 8 Linden St.

On a Sunday in June,
We had a barbecue on
Our uneven and skewed
Driveway.
Grass grew
Between the cracks—
We laughed.

Men cooked, drank,
At the grill,
Talked about
The Patriots and Bills.
The women set the table,
Sat in lawn chairs
With no cares.

The kids played
In the yard
And threw a ball,
But it didn't
Travel far
From the tree.

Carly Rae Jepsen

It's how the kids laughed at you—
Your daydreams,
Infatuation with fairies, Van
Morrison tunes.
After school
They went online
To forget
What they were.

Now, your intellect and breasts have formed.
Underneath your female peers think,
"How dare you
Break century-old chains.
The onus should
Be on men.

You're not an agent
For yourself or for us.
He must
Buy our drinks
For our time."

What I Think

She's afraid. Afraid the wind will blow, that
She doesn't deserve the polished stars' shine.
Afraid to explore what she doesn't know,
And to be part of a world real as mine.
Don't try: she won't accept a compliment,
Would rather slice off her ears and grin.
She doesn't recognize her own talents—
She's lost within, can't decide who she is.
But so am I—lost in a nebulous
Of smoky mirrors and half-hearted smiles,
Wandering through a black-hole existence
To a destination of endless turnstiles.
Dear, fear separates us, don't you see? But
I'm not waiting on someone not waiting for me.

North Shore Girl

She wore long,
Milky pants like
Sails from a sailboat
Whose waist
Fit snugly above her belly button and
Matched her
Cream-white heals. A
Saché
Tied in a bow acted
As a belt, securing
Her petit waistline.
To offset her
Lower attire,
A burgundy blouse
With vertical grooves
And a high collar
Covered
The contours
Of her throw-pillow breasts.

Over her blouse, a
Black cardigan
Draped from her shoulders, and
Her dark shade of
Lipstick accented the blouse. Her
Whitened teeth
Complemented the regality
Of her pearl earrings, and
Her symmetrical eyes possessed
A correlative quality to

Torghatten

Her chocolate, threadlike hair. Her
Sunglasses, like
Caviar saucers, rested
On top of her head.

Field Trip to *Brookline Booksmith*

My wheelchair descends a hill;
A Ferris wheel overlooks the sunset in Geneva.

A silver chariot arrives;
I am a rocket launching from Easton, Massachusetts.

A radio chants directions over voices;
Along the Charles, the window is a flipbook.

At the consumer library,
Gravity pulls my soles to the rabbit hole's end.

Down a concrete accordion,
Three youths carry me into Alexandria's cave.

Maxine's sugar-sprinkled, fried dough words
Whirl about, causing ideas to waltz my house of mirrors.

Back up the jagged edges;
Palms sweat and my heartbeat exceeds the speed limit.

Among a symphony of horns,
I boost into the chariot headed South.

On the way home, blackness spreads
Like jelly overhead as fireflies speed by.

Docila Rx

My senses are numb.
Where am I? I am here.

I see zombies on the horizon:
They didn't rise,
But they're the walking dead.

I can't escape, change my fate.
Inside I'm paralyzed, my skin the cage.
Tell the doc I said thanks.

I don't wear goth clothes,
Have tattoos, pierce my nose.
I act normal, you have nothing to fear.
Tell mom and dad that I said thanks.

In fifty years, if still I wake,
We were test subjects.

Just Kids

I. *The Athlete*

A thumb mashes an 'X' button;
The other thumb rotates on the ball of its joint.
A doppelgänger pirouettes on the screen.

Fingers coil around a pen
That glides across a glossy photo.
A storeowner rings up the price.

The athlete dives for a ball.
The president watches from a luxury box,
Pours a glass of whiskey.

* * *

II. *The Cancer Patient*

Lips form an asymmetrical grin;
Dull eyes widen.
Viewers tear, feel esophageal lumps.

Fingers coil around a rim,
Propel a set of wheels across a new floor.
God rings up the price.

Cameras fade, chemo comes into focus.
The president watches from an armchair.
An intern delivers a ratings report.

The Volunteer

In Uganda,
The volunteer helped
Those with H.I.V.,
Flirted
With natives
At a bar.

In China,
The volunteer fought
For freedoms like
At home, and
Gambled
Allowance away.

In Bolivia,
The volunteer taught
English; on weekends
Went surfing and
Learned the salsa.

In India,
The volunteer helped
Build a hospital, watched
A belly dance, and
Was fascinated by
The restrictive fashion.

Two Roads

Boston: such a fast-paced city.
Cars speed by
Like darts cutting through the air,
But too fast and too dangerous,
Until they hit their mark.

Boston's buildings construct urban valleys—
A Yosemite of concrete.

Gold, cinnamon hills
And tall graham grass
Stage the crisp backdrop of Montana.

Clouds cumulate
By the blurry car in Boston.
That road is not the one for me.
I belong in Montana, where it's not cloudy,
Nor mean or stubborn or busy or crazy.

I belong where the sun shines,

And the road is empty.

Assimilation

Help me.
Fix me.
Save me.
Make me
"Look good"
Like you.

Hurt me.
Fuck me.
Slice me.
Make me
"Feel good"
Like you.

Halt me.
Fault me.
De-salt me.
Make me
"Sound good"
Like you.

II. Eternal Chasm

Blink-Slack

There is a consciousness we gimps must endure, must alter. You
reading this may or may not understand that.

That consciousness is the reason that Danroy Henry's body Lay in a
New York City suburb.

It is the reason Jacob disregards candidates
Because their résumés have a female name on them.

Assumptions: insidious seeds, the reason
Passed-down declarations are reflexive as a blink.

You might think this far-fetched, think that we gimps have no quarrel,
That our struggle verges on paranoia because public opinion is on our
side,

But when a new business owner is forced to make a
Building handicdapped accessible—. We know why the dogs bark
at us.

I am not asking that you cut us slack. I am requesting You loosen the
lasso squeezing your mind—let it expand,

Blink different.

Gimp Romance

Flakes fell
On Saturday night.
Re-runs and Chinese, I
Felt a hole inside me, went
To the computer, hid
Behind a screen, talked
To a whore.
She wrote *I'll be there*
If you cover
My bus fare.

I opened the door
To her humming a tune
About dying young.
I said, "I'd rather live long
And be here."
She smiled. "The
Girls must love you."
We went to the couch,
Had some drinks
To prepare ourselves.
She stood like a statue,
Peeled her jeans off,
Pinched her shoulder blades,
So that her red top
Dropped and plopped
Like velvet frosting.

She sat on my lap,
Looked into my eyes and
Told me lies, then

Torghatten

I put it in her—
It was like a 'timeout',
And a visit

To the candy store
At the same time.
She blew my mind,
And said, "Where's my
Money, baby?" I replied,
"It's in my wallet
On the dresser."
She walked over. "I know
How much is there."
She thumbed my wallet, said,
"Sorry, hun, but I got a son."
And took all my cash
Down the fire escape.

The Disability Coordinator

Last weekend, she
Ran the Boston Marathon and
Donated her sponsors' money
To local schools.

She used to play
Basketball in college and
Joined The Peace Corps after.
She would listen to
Nigerian women share
Stories of rape and savagery.

As a mother, she
Always had an eye on
Her son at the park, and
Hosted parties with
Screaming kids while
She wrote.

On his first day
Of college, he rolled
Into her office, homesick,
Stomach churning, looking
For reassurance, someone
To share his experiences with.

To My Fellow Gimps

You will be led on.
Laughter will arise at
An undeserving quip.
The whites of eyes will
Grow, pupils will fixate
On you as you regale
Past stories or contribute
Meaningful insight, but
You're words are smoke—
Blown away with the wind.

Ableists are a confused watering can
Pouring acidic water
On the flower trying
To blossom—

Remember, some will stomp
The flower into oblivion.

They will hold the door open,
But won't stop it from closing.
They are no interested in
Pushing your wheelchair,
So don't burn clocks—
It's always your move.

They will satiate appetites
With warm tea.
They will digitize your smile,
Queue the violins.

C.R. Reardon

They will send you through wavelengths,
Smatter you on screens
To infiltrate sub-consciousnesses,
But your image will be filler

Like empty calories.

Misconceptions

She thinks I wrote the ethics book,
But only she knows why.
She thinks I'm deep as the ocean,
But the water is as high as her thigh.
Is that all right?

His buddies chastised him
When he took my money,
But he had a pair of aces—
I had a pair of threes.

I gave her coins to buy me
A drink in the store.
She handed me back my money
When she came out of the door.
She felt good.

The Beggar

I close my eyes, and see the whites of his—
December snow falling, falling.
Two blue pebbles dilate
Like the ocean waves that swell
In a Nor'Easter.

In summer, on my way
To night class,
I was in the downtown, by *Dunkin' Donuts*.
He came toward my car when he saw my
Handicapped placard in the front window.

Waiting for the light to turn green, he caught my eye Like a ghost
Hovering in the corner.
He asked for money,
Through my closed window.
Faintly, I heard him and locked the doors.
My window was now the sea wall separating
The mad from the sane.

His shirt was colored like a fire hydrant; his hat
The night and
Too big for him—it was on backward.
For some reason he
Had gray pillars under his armpits.
The light turned green. I started to move, and
Looked down. He was an amputee.

A brother of mine that I left behind for the wolves.

Rolling Backwards

When will this floor
Stop sloping,
My wheels keep rolling
Back?

My arms are flailing; I have no control.
If I grab my wheels
My fingers get chopped off in the spokes
Like a branch
Under a saw.

Where am I going?
I don't know.

My stomach feels
Black.

I see the image of my feet; think back
To when I was three.
Everything in front of me
Moves further away
Like the 'congratulations'
Of my youth.

Through a shot glass
I see a blurry picture frame.
My voicemail is silent,
My inbox blank.
On *Facebook* I watch friends' lives progress
And feel shame.

C.R. Reardon

When will this floor
Stop sloping,
My wheels keep rolling
Back?

I don't know.

7:00 AM Flight in Perdition

Wheels turning,
I roll down Route 1:
Chain stores dirty the sky.

The white lines put me to sleep
Along with the engine's hum.
Voices bicker on the radio.

I arrive at the airport.
Security pats me down—
Uniforms swab my seat, my back.

I'm strolling down the terminal.
A passing thigh rattles my frame.
I see my gate up ahead—

B17. I face a window:
White arms hold winged submarines
Floating on a sea of gray.

An army of plastic chairs taunt
As stragglers sink in them.
A bomb walks behind me.

Eyelid fixtures shine down.
A fire alarm offers reprieve.
Cable News laughs in its box.

A clear Starbucks cup is half-filled
With a brown, milky residue.
Fingers page a gossip magazine.

C.R. Reardon

On my left, I long the exit door—
Get me out of this place.

Indulge

I hope
You have thought of suicide,

Seen uneven edges of
An image amid black walls
That form a corner, a
Singular light shining
On your body in the fetal position—
You can see your breath
But not your face.

I hope
Your mind has ventured
To depths of depravity
Deep as a crevice on Everest.

I hope
You have pondered
The world without you—one
Less shadow to follow on the sidewalk.
Who will fill
The pews and how many?

I hope
You have dreamt of suicide.

I hope.

The Abyss

Water at your toes
Seeps through your skin.
Icy
Liquid infiltrates your veins.
A polar sensation rises,
With the bitter, translucent soup.
You can smell the morning.
Diaphragm shuts down;
You forget you have lower extremities.
Your faucet
Soon becomes flooded—
Taste the frigid.
Gasp, gasp;
See your last breath.
The clarity of life
Pushes upward through your line of vision.

North Shore Mall

Through this plastic, clogged artery
White gavels fixate on me
Because they don't see anyone
Like me on their screens.

Here, silk illuminates
Windows and silver drenches
The *Coach* store.
Abercrombie and Fitch
Harbors soft individuals
Like a Banana Republic.

Entertainment Tonight looms in a box
Over my head like a chandelier:
"Look at me. Look at me."
Cheers to natural disasters and sex scandals.
The host's voice
Echoes through this lard-laced artery.

Here come the high school students.
I'm rolling against the current.

Yay!

The Satire

"The idea
Of children fighting to the death
Is outrageous, and
Should not be celebrated or
Profited from—
Death is not a sport."

On an autumn
Saturday morning, a
Family drives to a field:
Parents sit on
Creaky, warped bleachers,
Siblings run around, and
Cheerleaders cheer
While Trevor launches
His helmeted-head at
His opponent's.

Eric and Dylan shot
Their classmates at Columbine.
Then Seung-Hui Cho
Committed the deadliest
Shooting by a single gunman
At Virginia Tech, and
Adam Lanza blasted
Twenty-three children
With four glocks in
The safe haven of
New Town, CT.

Lily sits in her high chair

Torghatten

At the dinner table, sees news clips
In grainy night-vision on TV.
A flash dazzles and
Gets her attention while shoveled
Soft food. In twenty years
She'll realize that
She watched the murder of her peer.

Dennis's Tears

Dennis came back to college,
Was a candidate for the Heisman Trophy,
Donated his time to kids, his studies.

An Oregon duck hiked the football,
A pack of wildcats hunted

Dennis. He tried to juke, he tried
To shift, but his weak knee drifted

Past healthy,
Snapping his ligament.

Dennis's tears formed black pools on his cheek—
They were broadcast to millions.

Vanish did his dream, his ticket, his meal.

I hope ratings met their demands
When Erin reported fears no family needs clear—
You need sleep now and think about Dennis's tears.

Sisters

A cold front
In the upper atmosphere
Passes over an
Unseasonable warm front, stirring
The air, producing
A twister that splitces in two.

Inside one twister,
A digital thread lengthens—
A snake
Eats its tail.
Along the thread,
Teeth of wind-up
Monkey dolls
Chatter.

Inside the other,
A digital thread lengthens—
A snake
Eats its tail.
Along the thread
Fingers on a broken
Piano Player
Shuck-and-jive.

The sisters destroy all in their path.

Dear Patrick
For the Tillman Family

Dear Patrick,
I'm sorry we did that—
Put a value on your life.
I wish we could go back.

It's too late.
He said, "Abraham,
Kill me a son."
And we did just that.

Dear Patrick,
Will you forgive us?
I don't blame you if you say, "No."

Millennial Whispers

Would you kill
Someone because your boss
Demanded it, or if
Your parents nodded
With approval?

Will the local news
Gather at doorsteps—
Cameras monitoring windows—
If such a blasphemous
Question is asked?

Would this poem
Cease to exist
If a bearded man existed?

Would the Constitution and
Declaration of Independence
Vanish
Like sand in
A windy desert?

Someone pulled the trigger.

Even Angels Get Shot

"Don't blame me,"
Says the officer to the reporter.
"I was just doing my job,
Enforcing the laws, and
The laws said Jared Lee could
Own a gun—it's not arson.
Sorry if I sound defensive, but there's
No way we could've foreseen his motives."

"It wasn't I,"
Says the college girl, sipping
A *Venti*, sheltered from the world.
"It's the Republicans' fault, they
Don't care about mental health,
Just assault rifles and wealth. People die
In their Mideast war every day,
So how is this different anyways?"

"What did I do?"
Says the slick-haired comedian
In New York City. "I'm just trying
To get a laugh, report the facts—
I don't see any crime in that." He argues
While charming guests, aiming
His rhetoric at the opposing view,
Preaching to all his virtue.

"It's a shame."
Says Bill, finishing
His beer, watching wrestling,

Torghatten

Cheering, "Yeah!"
"That gal should have screamed, if she
Did, someone could have wrestled that clown
To the ground before he got off those rounds,
But she had to be a strong female, and
Act all nice—stupid
Democrat, paid the price."

Tragedy in Tucson
Started the news report.
The anchors accused the lone wolf
Because he had all the 'warning signs',
Compared it to Virginia Tech, Columbine.
They pretended to point the finger
At themselves,
But they didn't have time to delve.
So, they put pundits on a split-screen
And asked what this meant politically.

"Don't apportion blame,"
Says the ex-governor, and goes on
To use a quote blaming society.
Then blames this tragedy on the 'apolitical' Jared Lee.
No-sir-ee, it had nothing to do
With cross-hairs she put over Gabby's county
Because Gabby voted for a bill
That she believed would help, but
Not in this 'exceptional country'
'That is the light of the world.'

"This was part of God's plan,"
The housewife says on her cell
To a friend—they both mean well—

But they ain't in the hospital bed
With a bullet hole inside their head
Wondering how life will be—They're
On the golden side of destiny.

Who shot Gabby Giffords?
We all did.

Emilie

Blonde hair like the moon's glow,
Eyes stone blue with ivory skin.
She told Robbie in Portuguese,
"Eu te amo." And gave him a kiss.

Alyssa's mouth is a frozen ridge.
Her brain has frostbite.
Let her sob on the couch—
You amplify the noise in her head.
Adam went to the shooting range
With his mother—she was a survivalist.

He stole her AR-15 and Saiga just in case,
Shot her twice, and went to school.

Queasy City

I have a pain in my stomach.
Not a moment-by
Moment pang like repeated
Stabs, but rather a
Slow churning of acid
In my gut like a storm brewing.

Cathleen always wanted to be a teacher.
Her freckled face, brown
Hair, and toothy smile
Greeted the loner in
Congested halls, spoke
Cordially to the stoner,
The popular kids, the athletes
Who had to take her math test after school—
At age twenty-four, she
Was one of them.

On Wednesday, Cathleen was friendly to the wrong student—
Friendliness is a two-way street.

Paul had walked to a nearby
Wholesale store,
Bought a boxcutter, and,
After the students had left for the day,
Followed Cathleen into the bathroom,
Slit her throat,
Folded the blood-spattered body
Into a receptacle, and
Dumped it in the woods.

Torghatten

The police found Paul walking
In the breakdown lane on Route 128.
He was sentenced to life in prison.
He was fourteen.

My stomach hurts.

Neda

In a land where women are covered
With a sheet, Buried to their breasts
While standing, and pelted with stones,
A young rebel, who never liked authority,
Smiled like she always smiled.

Her room
Was like any young woman's:
A poster of a desired man against
Muted purple walls. On her bed,
Sat stuffed animals, and on her messy desk
A stack of books towered.
Her TV reflected the cover of Bronte's *Wuthering Heights*.
Sometimes she looked in her mirror and danced
To an Arab pop song or Western music.

After two semesters at university, she
Dropped out, but while there, wore pink high heels,
Red lipstick, and nail polish despite the guards
And other women telling her she couldn't.
Beauty was a danger to them.

She became a tour guide in Turkey, wore
A short jean skirt with white fringe. She
Yearned to escape the sight of women in
Black burkas and dresses at the beach.

Back I n familiar territory,
She marched for freedom with thousands of others:
Her mother pleaded for her to return home, but
This Middle Eastern rogue replied on her cell phone,

Torghatten

"If I don't, who will?"
On June 20th, 2009 she was shot
In the heart, blood seeped through dirt streets:
In Tehran's sun she died with open eyes,
With open eyes.

She was my sister, your sister: she
Is you.

Wiretapped Land

In this wiretapped land
'Individuals' finger the
Alphabet, have sex with
Droids, and are all about the i
Phone.

Through the static,
Mass panic, I see
Parasitic pundits, critics
That are
Manic, frantic slaves,
Trudging through
Days to
Corporate graves with price tags.
It seems
Nepotism is all the rage,
And taking orders is
Part of the game, at least
That's what the broker will say
As he snorts coc
And ties the prostitute
To the bedpost.
What about
The families whose
Kids brush their teeth
In gas station bathrooms
Before they go to school
Where books teach them about
The penal system, and
Not the feudal system
They're living in?

Golden Eagle Terrain
A surrealist Sestina

On Skittish Sunday, wheels rolled on an unraveling hijab, Traversed
a sliver of silver bridge into a screen—
Heard gunfire and applause, saw an electronic dawn.
The director choreographed blue and white titans,
Took video of the crime scene, put the camera on a treadmill.
Wind-up mice scurried below eighteenth-century portraits.

Sulfur boils bubble on souls; who will paint their portraits? The soot-
soaked puppet man in a tie is in need of a hijab.
His toxic paper is still craved by the nymph on a treadmill. He's your
neighbor pouring benzene through a screen
Onto skyscraper stalks producing a pride of jelly-rolled titans.
A mail tube sends fireworks underground—it's a new dawn!

This business grid mines mystics for capital in the dawn
While glasses with limestone lenses look at their portraits, But all the
viewers' senses are tirelessly assaulted by titans, So rabid-eyed groves
stammer to frosting factories in hijabs.
If you get on your knees and leer through limestone screens
You'll see the titans are just ants marching on a treadmill.

Lies float on a twisty wind and run on a corroding treadmill. They
pass through PCV and proliferate in our midnight dawn.
Clog the gramophone, burn all the 'roided seeds and screens. Let the
Sun fuck you, be the painter of landscapes and portraits.
Forget fire trucks and Twitter, 'made in the U.S.A.', and hijabs.
We're living in 1984 so I'll be swimming with Galileo on Titan.

Leather-skinned boy scouts castigate their fellow titans
And cast them off to travel on a highway that is a two-hour treadmill

While they obfuscate their fear of cooties like they do their fear of
hijabs.
Knuckles and flying skeletons imprint warnings: a jackknife dawn
Where citizens fertilize rolling hill cognition—the world's new
portrait—
Instead of airbrushing Yosemite, watching life's aureole through a
screen.

Bloodline forms cover the floor; the choir is protected by a screen.
On a fiendish construction, there are no shadows among skeevy
titans.
Those who committed cerebral, cathedral hacks are given portraits
While paper sweat is heaved in a wood-chipper that rains on a
treadmill.
Let ink melt into the ether, and hemp burn in this rare Earth dawn
Where a brown-skinned woman on a crucifix wears nothing but a
hijab.

Flocks foam for four-inch screens, to be seen, to rampage on
treadmills
And emulate the coin-lined titans they decry in this millennial dawn
While the portraits of camouflaged kings look out on piled hijabs.

We Are Not What We Were

World, don't wait for us
To stop fighting civil wars.

World, don't wait for us
To create an industry.

World, don't wait for us
To purify your tears.

World, don't wait for us
To close the hole in the sky.

World, don't wait for us
To cultivate galaxies.

World, don't wait for us
To cure you. We can't cure ourselves.

III. Keep the Faith

Leaving Dodge

I pack my bag,
Hitch it on my wheelchair
And roll out of my room.
I ain't looking back, keeping
My eyes like jacks
Glued to the tops of my shoes
So I don't scrape the wall.
And when I reach
That door, I'll say "What for?"
Then I'll get on my way.

No more rush hour,
Parked at the Revere theaters,
Staring at the *Kappy's Liquors* sign.
I'm tired of snow,
So I must go, Maybe
I'll find a girl.
We'll dream of Barcelona,
Fields of four-leaf clovers,
And go anywhere
But here.

Modern Man

Dressed in plaid shorts,
You wear a collared shirt—
"It's not pink, it's salmon."
You put on cologne,
Brush your gelled hair with a comb,
Text on your cell phone and
Look for acknowledgment.

Sitting at the bar,
She eyes you from afar,
Dreams you're a doctor and
Waits for you to buy her a drink.
You tell her about your scars and
Trophies, but
Don't reveal too much.
You want an aura of mystery—
According to the movie.

You get her drunk,
Take her back to your place.
She is gorgeous and shaved,
As is your chest, nether
Region.

The Chameleon's Paper Smile

Long legs walk in
Dripping with sin
Not for me,
Not for me.

Plump lips smile, a
Tongue sticks out in jest:
It hurts,
Breaks me.

A nimble hand
Strokes reverie-hair;
I wander
Jade eyes.

I don't deserve
Her firm body.
I don't.
I don't?

She makes other girls
Feel like untouched pies
At a bake sale.

I know she thinks
Highly of me, but
Won't act, she
Won't act.

Murdering Cinderella

Doris held the wine glass's
Bottom, the stem
Between her middle and ring fingers.
She placed the glass on
A chestnut coffee table,
Across from Candice's.
Doris wore jeans, sat
On her leg on an
Ivory couch in her apartment.
The lights dimmed;
Doris stroked Candice's prairie hair.
Candice's nerves fluttered, glands secreted at
The sight of Doris's buxom curves, her
Jet-black hair cut straight
At the bangs, and her pink
Glossed lips. Doris eased
Candice's mind by
Kissing her while holding her face.
Candice felt
Empowered, courageous, and
Put her hand on Doris's waist,
Then slid them up
Doris's lavender Izod
To her augmented breasts,
Which Doris felt had augmented
Her confidence. Doris moved
Her hand down Candice's black dress,
Pulled the skirt up, underwear off,
And inserted her fingers.

Years later,

Torghatten

Doris wore an apron
In the kitchen over a
Polka-dot sundress. She
Wanted simplicity,
She wanted to serve.
Candice modeled, but knew
The end was near, so
She started a filming
And photography agency—
Doris consulted (She knew people
In the business). Most days
Doris would write or draw at home.
She would watch her favorite TV shows—
Ellen and *Guiding Light*.
By now,
Candice had dyed her hair pink
And accrued
Several tattoos
Like Barbie.
Doris worried
About Candice, her fragile frame,
The stress of work—
They didn't need the money,
But some people have to keep moving
Like tectonic plates.

They are in their fifties now.
Doris has back pain; Candice
Drives her to physical therapy
Twice a week (Doris had
Never learned to drive). When
Doris does her exercises at home
Candice helps her.
Candice has become

Mentally unstable, but is
On a minimal dose
Of medicine—Doris does not
Trust pharmaceuticals. But
Every morning she puts Candice's pills
On the table with a glass
Of orange juice, and when
Candice comes home, Doris has supper
Waiting.
They have seen it all,
Walked through the desert together.
They sit across from each other
At the kitchen table,
Look into each other's eyes,
And hold hands.

Iris

Every spring, it breathes;
In the winter, it wilts.

No human eye can detect
It choking on
The element its
Inhaling like someone's
Lungs popping from
Having their nose pinched and
Ingesting an oxygen tank.

Like you,
Like me,
It is an organism—
That pale blue dot.

The Glory of Limits

They say 'the sky is the limit.'
They're right.
There's a universe
Beyond the blue.

We are here
Due to luck.
The good news
Is we are stuck.

'The sky is the limit'—
That leaves us a lot of space.

Refugee Grains

Humid air grazed skin;
Winter's sun beamed in the glass cradle.
Green isles were splattered with turquoise grains—
Flapping, bordered in black.
These convulsing grains captivated glossy eyes
Like a push-lawn mower's spinning blade caches grass. Nature's
cycles had not killed this creature
Or faded its colors, but
Instead, pumped it full of anatomy:
It fought through its gray cocoon
Like fluorescence emanating from stone.

Naked, it only had cold mornings and
Myopic heads observing sideways
To look forward to.

A photograph catches
Me smiling as
The refugee grains fluttered free.

Chess Lesson at Linkin Park

The king is useless,
The queen shamefully ignored.
Rooks are self-constricted—
The game's narrow-minded pieces.
Bishops are always angling
For a victory. Knights
Seem harmless, but watch out
For their clever movements.

It is the all-powerful pawns
That dictate where
The other pieces move. Pawns
Are the first line of defense,
The first to mobilize.

The player must realize
The fingertips' power.

Train Ride into Boston, Epiphany on the Subway

They don't care about you, child.
They don't care your wheels spun for
Twenty-six minutes over cracked
Concrete concealing mangled tree roots.
They don't care that you held your breath
While you sped over gaps
Between pavement and tracks
So you could board the train on the correct side.

They don't know
You left home
Hoping your adventure went smoothly—
Spontaneity: an adrenaline concoction.
Out a dirtied window, your eyes glided along
Electrical wires overlooking a marsh
From the carved space where you sat.

They don't know
You punched a silver moon in North Station, opening A door with
two windows framed in evergreen.
You cascaded left, then right
Down a plastic-tiled ramp, and
Punched another moon
Offering you to urban wolves:
They look just like you but they
Stand.

Up the sidewalk's incline,
Through beige automatic doors, left
To an elevator that delivers you

Below street level
To a lair where subway cars
Slink in and out like steel caterpillars.
A green one arrives and a woman
In a blue uniform smiles:
She sifts through her keys
That jingle as she puts one in
A keyhole and turns it.
A mechanical black shelf eases out,
Lowering to the warning strip.
"Where are you going?"
"Cleveland Circle." You roll on board.
She doesn't know.

Once you back into the only spot
For you,
You observe:
The Puerto Rican woman with a frilly
White bonnet over her carriage
Talks in an avocado tongue to a
Friend whose fingers coil a pole.
A mahogany girl hunches like
A geranium over an English textbook,
Studying each word with her spectacles.
An Asian man slouches:
His hat's brim points Northeast.
Unkempt hair squeezes down,
Invading his sun-shades.
His sneakers' tongues stick out at
The white man with a shaved head
And two chins. His work papers
Seethe in a bag on his shoulder, and his
Stubby fingers, sweaty palms are trapped

Torghatten

In his pockets. A Cadillac
Out the window chases you.

They don't know, they don't care:
It's a Coco-cloud type feeling.

February 12th, 2015

Dad's weathered hands pushed down,
My front wheels lifted—
A horse
On its hind legs.

Through
Sugary grains, we sifted
To the car amidst
City lights. My boot
Slipped on black ice—
He lifted me.

We turned
Onto our street:
Behemoth snow piles
Formed a gauntlet like
A fantasy scene.

He pushed me up
The lightly coated ramp.
Mom opened the golden door,
Turned the light on.
Dad moved me far
Enough in the house
To close the door behind him.

She, in her pajamas,
Had a rag
In hand, and bent over
As she wiped my caster wheels,
Brushed off the

Torghatten

Front of my big tires.
Then, like a magician's
Slight of hand, mom
Passed the rag to dad,
Around me.

He wiped down
The back of my tires:
I was dead-eyed, my
Body like
My wheelchair. Like a
Car in a
Carwash, he gradually
Pushed me, both of my parents
Wiping sections of my tires.

After, dad took
His winter coat off,
Went to bed, and said:
"Keep the faith."
Mom helped me
Take off my coat, brought
Me a Coke.

Admiration Not Love

I will find Griselda
Who bestows a life free of stigma.
She will live her life
Like the human that she is.

She sees the goodness in me,
And thinks independently.
There is a nobility about her
That the king does not behold.

Genitals aren't just for birds;
'Love' and 'marriage' are just words.
She is a subject and not an object—
A subject I study long and hard.

The only war she'll fight is for me.
She's quick-witted and artsy.
She can absorb a joke and project one.
She knows the world in which she lives.

She's motherly without the mother
She speaks and doesn't mutter.
She spends her days with me because she wants to
And I do the same.

Chemiluminescence

I might be a light bulb,
Not the most well made, but
My wheels spin for you.
I will pioneer the way.

Your touch heats this steel.
Your phosphorous smile,
Just like a soul's spoke,
Glows the night
Tonight.

We are neon wheels.

Rhyolite, Melted

Dust blew over barren ground.
The clouds were gray, but
Split to reveal an azure boulevard.
The zephyr said, "Isn't it glorious?"

A wrist shackled by a watch;
A smart phone and calendar: you put a
'For Sale' sign on your brain. Mercy cried,
"Don't be technology's casualty."

Go forth, roam
North, South, East and West.
Hear the ocean sing,
Watch birds soar.

Limbo

A Snickers bar
Dangles out of reach;
I feel the watermelon dawn
And know I'm nature's pawn.

Highway under my wheels,
A black hole behind me;
Its swirling wind rips my skin
As it tries to suck me in.

That's where you'll find me,
Somewhere between
The rays of light and the dark of night—
Living.

Torghatten[1]

AB 's ain't bringing hate— [2]
They didn't burn my people at the stake.
They just have a subcutaneous disdain
When they see my gimpy face:
I get to cut lines, live off government aid
While they're 9-5 provides checks and self-worth— They complain.
When you're the last minority
On a list of minorities,
You have rivers to cross,
Rivers to shape.

When peddlers preach eugenic solutions
The 'inspirational' illusion
Comes to a conclusion. Gimps
Are the first to go—
We're the weakest link, you know?
We're worth the price of air,
Even though we breathe 'how-to'
And hold ideas never shared.

AB's hold doors for us, think
Whores are the answer for us—
That will fill
What's empty. So, gimps,
Give *them* your pity because
They only know one reality.
They believe the myth of equality.
I wish they'd subscribe to
Humanity.

Torghatten

Gimps ain't going to the mountain top,
We jetting through it—
Ain't looking back, ain't wasting time on it.